Dr. Shields' conversation around generosity was akin to a north star pointing out to us the way to travel our life that really matters. The compactness of his content and the heart of the writer came together as a personal conversation from one who cares deeply about others. I felt as if the conversations were personal notes written just for me, and I am sure that others will feel likewise.

−Clifton L. Taulbert
Pulitzer Nominee
President of the Freemount Consultancy
Author of "Eight Habits of the Heart"

Ric Shields has given us twenty-seven one-minute lessons that encourage, convict, and inspire us to be genuine and generous givers. It is a rich resource for pastors and Christian leaders, and I am confident you will be blessed as you read, reflect, and respond to these valuable lessons.

−Phil Taylor
Senior Pastor
Carbondale Assembly of God

Learning these practical principles on giving as a teenager over thirty-five years ago from the author has been key to the foundation and success of our company. Starting our business with just $500 (everything we had), we also pledged to give that much monthly to this very ministry having no idea how we would be able to afford it. Over twenty-five years later, we have never missed a gift, and our total giving has only continued to grow. Now we have a multimillion-dollar business, and God continues to increase *"exceedingly and abundantly above all things"* with these principles at work in our lives and business every day.

−Joel David Wiland
Founder, J. David Jewelry
Ministry in Retail and Business

Through the years, my brother and his wife, Ric and Sheila, have found meaningful ways to connect resources to need. The calculation never starts with the cost, but it is driven by the outcomes they envision. This book gives practical guidance and meaningful instruction to those who have determined to make their lives count through compassionate living and giving.

–Mike Shields
Director
Christian Training Network, Int'l

I felt as though I was staring at myself through one thousand mirrors, each causing me to think harder, surrender more, and be more intentional about this thing called generosity. After nearly twenty-nine years spent in military service, one of my prevailing thoughts is *How do I loosen my grip on this life to better give myself away?* This book will help me with that assignment!

–Chaplain (Colonel) Ken Revell
U.S. Army, Retired

These modern-day giving parables reveal the generous character of God. This must-read resource will help you develop a heart of generosity and challenge you to live—and give—like never before.

–Pastor Elizabeth Farina
Stewardship Coach

Generous Measures is a very thought-provoking collection of teachings about becoming more motivated givers. Ric has combined real-life stories and illustrations with Scripture, helping us to exercise our faith to give generously from our hearts.

–Lowell D Nystrom
Cofounder and Senior VP of TSI Inc., Retired
Author of *Giving and Growing in God: Lessons on Giving from God's Word*

Dr. Shields unique method of storytelling can inspire, impart biblical truths, and give new spiritual insights. "Generous Measures" is a much-needed tool within reach for ministers – not only to share with their congregations but to also apply in their personal lives.

–Sameh Sadik, PhD
Executive Director
Operation Serve International

This wonderful book not only shares principles and stories regarding generosity, but I have watched Ric live it out in his own life. This book is filled with nuggets of truth that will inspire you. Get copies of it to pass on to others. It's a great investment.

–MICHAEL GOLDSMITH
Founding Pastor
The Ridge at Broken Arrow

My wife, Judy, and I have been a part of the Shields' very effective missions ministry from its earliest days. Most recently, I have been blessed to be able to encourage Dr. Shields as he has developed and published this book. I am sure you will find the following pages to be most encouraging.

–NORMAN R LINDSAY, D. MIN
Alaska Ministry Network Officer, Retired

GENEROUS MEASURES

One–Minute Lessons with a Lifetime of Value

Inspire generosity!

Ric Shields

BY
RIC SHIELDS Prov. 22:9

WORD & SPIRIT
PUBLISHING

CONTENTS

DEDICATION

To my wife, Sheila, and our children, Travis and Tara. Together, we have learned what it means to live and give with generosity in our hearts. We may not have figured it all out, but we continue to grow in the *"grace of giving"* (2 Corinthians 8:7 NIV).

And to those who have modeled generosity by their support of the ministries of DoorWays. Your love and support have blessed us and touched the lives of countless others all over the world.

"Now to him who is able to do immeasurably more than all we ask or imagine, according to his power that is at work within us, to him be glory in the church and in Christ Jesus throughout all generations, for ever and ever! Amen" (Ephesians 3:20–21 NIV).

REFLECTIONS

The stories in this book were written with church and ministry leaders in mind. Each story is exactly two hundred words long and can be read aloud in one minute or less. I hope these stories will help provide valuable illustrations about generosity for both leaders and followers, for both receivers and distributors, and for those who may struggle with the grace of giving.

A handful of friends joined my wife, Sheila, and me to begin the ministry of **DoorWays®** in 1990. We started with nothing more than a two-drawer filing cabinet on loan to us from our church. We had no other supplies or equipment and have been on the receiving end of generosity ever since.

While we still have a fairly small operation, God has helped us to do big things. We have sponsored hundreds of Bible college students in Argentina, Cuba, Bangladesh, Russia, and Bolivia. Our ministry teams have helped to build and update Bible schools, churches, and children's homes and have provided disaster relief in the Dominican Republic, in Indonesia, in Haiti, and in New Orleans following Hurricane Katrina. We have joined with other ministries to provide health and dental care, optical exams, glasses, haircare, groceries, and school supplies to thousands in Mexico and Egypt. Over two hundred freshwater wells have been provided on church properties in the impoverished country of Bangladesh. Nearly 1,400 team members have joined us on 150 outreaches to twenty-four nations on six continents.

Simply Sisters® (a ministry arm of **DoorWays®**) is a small group of caring women who show their love in the things they do. Whether they are helping people deal with depression, divorce, grief, loss, or illness, they strive to show the love of Jesus to those who need it most. They assemble care baskets with things they make, they purchase, or are donated, and then they deliver or mail the baskets with notes of encouragement. They also pray for those who receive the gifts and believe the Lord will touch their hearts through the love sent their way. Over six hundred boxes and baskets and up to three tons of items have been given through this ministry to others at no cost to the recipients.

There's more to be told, but there is a limited amount of space. Suffice it to say that we have learned about generosity as both the receivers and distributors of resources. We have found the joy that comes from giving, even when others have advised us we were in over our heads. The Lord has always provided, even when we didn't know how or where the provisions would come from.

Undoubtedly, there are others more generous than us. Their stories inspire and challenge us and help us to learn from their example. Please consider writing your story and sending it to us. If you can, keep it to two hundred words or less. Perhaps your story will appear in a follow-up edition to this book.

–RIC SHIELDS
DoorWays®
PO Box 2023, Broken Arrow, OK 74013
Email: info@doorways.cc

HOW TO USE THIS BOOK

Personal Reflection and Sharing

Four questions follow each story.

1. How does this story challenge me?
2. How might I change this story in order to make it more relevant to my situation?
3. How can I reduce this story into one short sentence?
4. How do I hope others might respond to this story?

Responding to each of those questions will make the story personal to you. Give yourself permission to increase the value of a story by changing it to best fit your context. The added value of your personalized story will provide a better opportunity for your listeners to make a direct application to their lives, too.

Congregational or Group Sharing

Week 1: Share a story with those in your congregation or group.

Week 2: Follow up by reminding others of the previous week's story, and ask for their personal reflections. Has anyone had the opportunity to put the lesson learned from the story into practice? Was there a resulting experience?

GENEROUS MEASURES

A friend once gave us good advice to help avoid a quarrel between our two children. She suggested that sharing a soft drink or a candy bar would be easier if we allowed one to split and the other to choose. It sometimes made the task of splitting a tedious one. In our home, it could mean using a ruler or scale for accuracy. If the split was not exactly equal, the splitter could quickly become the loser, and the chooser would be the winner. More often than not, neither came out ahead of the other.

Thankfully, when they grew into adults, our kids didn't feel the need to bring that practice along with them. Both are generous and not likely to get caught losing sleep over a few dollars owed by a friend.

How should we measure our giving? With grace and generosity as a guide, give more than you planned, and you will experience the freedom it brings. When grace and generosity are our measure, we will be sure to find them coming back to us.

"Give, and it will be given to you....For with the measure you use, it will be measured to you" (Luke 6:38 NIV).

MY TAKEAWAYS:

1. How does this story challenge me?

2. How might I change this story in order to make it more relevant to my situation?

3. How can I reduce this story into one short sentence?

4. How do I hope others might respond to this story?

FLEETING TREASURES

*H*er family had spent much of their adult lives as missionaries in Central America. In her spare time, she developed an interest in antique tea sets. Her one-of-a-kind collection represented some of the finest sets of pots, cups, and saucers. Some were exquisitely hand-painted; others, fashioned from fine porcelain, felt delicate to the touch.

It wasn't the monetary investment—it was the emotional attachment she felt to each piece. Her family and the occasional housekeeper knew not to concern themselves with dusting the collection. Should something ever happen to a piece, she would have only herself to blame.

And that's what happened. One day, while carefully moving the collection to the kitchen for cleaning, she tripped with a tray full of her treasures. Her beautiful collection became nothing more than porcelain shards and splinters.

"I was placing an enormous investment of time and energy into my collection. As difficult as it was, that moment set me free."

Jesus said in Matthew 6:19–21, *"Do not store up for yourselves treasures on earth....But store up for yourselves treasures in heaven....For where your treasure is, there your heart will be also"* (NIV).

Earthly treasures may disappoint us; eternal investments will greet us there.

MY TAKEAWAYS:

1. How does this story challenge me?

2. How might I change this story in order to make it more relevant to my situation?

3. How can I reduce this story into one short sentence?

4. How do I hope others might respond to this story?

BLESSED TO GIVE

*B*aksheesh is a word often heard in the Middle East and Southern Asia. It is used to describe tipping, charitable giving, and even bribes. Most often, *baksheesh* is "rudely demanded and graciously received with little or no services rendered."* When a person requests *baksheesh* as a gift, it comes with the implication that one is blessed for the opportunity to give to another.

It seems Jesus would tend to agree, and the apostle Paul took that teaching to heart in his farewell address to the Ephesian elders in Acts 20. Looking back at his time of self-supported ministry and giving to the poor, he recited Jesus' saying: *"It is more blessed to give than to receive"* (verse 35).

How can that be? It seems the person on the receiving end is the one being blessed while the individual doing the giving is being used.

Proverbs 22:9 (NIV) says, *"The generous will themselves be blessed, for they share their food with the poor"*. Knowing the Lord will bless a generous heart gives us the confidence that we will have more than enough in the days ahead. God's blessing will surely come to those who give and bless others in the process.

---

* *Testaments of Time: The Search for Lost Manuscripts and Records,* New York (1966), 367.

MY TAKEAWAYS:

1. How does this story challenge me?

2. How might I change this story in order to make it more relevant to my situation?

3. How can I reduce this story into one short sentence?

4. How do I hope others might respond to this story?

CONTENTED LIVING

*P*rior to receiving an offering, some pastors encourage their congregation to make a corporate, verbal affirmation. It is not quite a prayer, but they declare together a belief for jobs, better jobs, raises, bonuses, sales, settlements, inheritances, rebates and checks in the mail, gifts, surprises, debts paid off, decreased expenses, blessing, and increase. Any of these would be welcomed; all of them would be a miracle.

Though Scripture teaches it, there appears to be no room in the proclamation for a statement regarding stewardship or personal responsibility. There is no place for one to ask forgiveness for their self-centeredness or spending beyond their means.

Scripture teaches that godliness is not *"a means to financial gain."* Rather, we are taught that *"godliness with contentment is great gain"* (1 Timothy 6:5–6 NIV).

What would happen if we asked the Lord to help us better understand how to properly use the resources entrusted to us? The gospel's parable of the ten talents should be a guide. Jesus teaches that those who have been faithful with little will be given even more.

Until we have learned how to be the best managers of what we have, it seems unwise that we should ask for even more.

MY TAKEAWAYS:

1. How does this story challenge me?

2. How might I change this story in order to make it more relevant to my situation?

3. How can I reduce this story into one short sentence?

4. How do I hope others might respond to this story?

A GIFT FROM THE HEART

*A*s a young minister, I adopted a theory on giving heard from the time I was a child. Countless pastors, teachers, and ministry leaders had used the phrase, and it seemed reasonable that it should become a part of my teaching on giving, too.

The idea was to make people responsible givers by helping them to view their tithe as if it were a debt. The mantra went like this: "Paying your tithe is like paying a bill you owe." Tithing needed to be nothing more than a reflexive action. When the telephone or utility bill arrived, I sent a check and paid the bill on time. With that same, unemotional response, I paid my tithe.

I did it religiously—and that was the problem.

The apostle Paul wrote in 2 Corinthians 9:7 about proper attitudes in giving: *"Each of you should give what you have decided in your heart to give, not reluctantly or under compulsion, for God loves a cheerful giver* (NIV)".

God desires for us to give our tithe as an expectant response from a grateful heart. When it becomes less than that, we miss the entire point and risk the loss of His blessing when we give.

MY TAKEAWAYS:

1. How does this story challenge me?

2. How might I change this story in order to make it more relevant to my situation?

3. How can I reduce this story into one short sentence?

4. How do I hope others might respond to this story?

THE MONKEY TRAP

*A*re you smarter than a monkey?

Monkey trappers in North Africa have devised a clever method of catching their prey. They fill empty gourds with nuts and firmly fasten them to tree branches. Each gourd has a small hole just large enough to allow an unsuspecting monkey to stick its extended forepaw through.

When a hungry monkey discovers the treasure inside a gourd, he quickly grasps a handful of the prize. But it's actually a trap because the hole is too small for him to withdraw his clenched fist. The poor monkey doesn't have enough sense to simply open his hand, let it go, and be free. Rather than release the newly found treasure and escape, he foolishly refuses and is easily taken captive.

What things are you holding so tightly in your life that they make you a captive? Let go before it's too late and you become the servant instead of the master.

Jesus taught us in Matthew 6:19–21, *"Do not store up for yourselves treasures on earth, where moth and rust destroy, and where thieves break in and steal. But store up for yourselves treasures in heaven...for where your treasure is, there your heart will be also."*

MY TAKEAWAYS:

1. How does this story challenge me?

2. How might I change this story in order to make it more relevant to my situation?

3. How can I reduce this story into one short sentence?

4. How do I hope others might respond to this story?

REAPING WHAT WE SOW

*S*pringtime! Cold temperatures inch away. The sun rises earlier each morning and retreats later at day's end. Trees bud, grass grows, and flowers splash their colors like crayons opened in a kindergarten classroom.

Near the first sign of spring, seeds are planted with the expectation of an ample harvest. Beans, tomatoes, carrots, and peas join other vegetables and herbs filling pots and plots.

At the end of each row, gardeners often affix seed packages to sticks to remind them what should be expected as seeds begin to sprout. And exactly what do the gardeners expect? They clearly anticipate plants with pods of peas where peas were planted and tomato plants where tomato seeds were planted.

The apostle Paul wrote in Galatians 6:7, *"A man reaps what he sows,"* and he added this instruction in verse 9: *"Let us not become weary in doing good, for at the proper time we will reap a harvest if we do not give up"* (NIV).

When you give, do it with a sense of expectancy—just like you would if you were planting a seed. A harvest lies ahead, and God will be faithful to bring all you need at just the right time.

MY TAKEAWAYS:

1. How does this story challenge me?

2. How might I change this story in order to make it more relevant to my situation?

3. How can I reduce this story into one short sentence?

4. How do I hope others might respond to this story?

TAKING CHANCES

I've heard it many times. A person spends their last dollar buying a lottery ticket. After all, they can't win if they don't play. Since someone has to win the big jackpot, it might as well be them. And, if they are lucky enough to be the big winner, half of their winnings will be given to charities or their local church.

Somehow, it seems they may have their financial plans backward. Statistics show that people have a 1 in 2.32 million chance of being struck by lightning, while winning the Powerball comes with the astronomically high odds of 1 in 292.2 million. This means that one would be over 125 times more likely to be struck by lightning than to win the lottery. It seems that not playing the lottery might be the safest and most likely way to be two dollars richer at the end of the day.

When we wait to give until we have the money to do it, we will consistently run out of money before we give. Worse yet, we will miss the blessing of the Lord that comes from the obedience of giving.

"Give, and it will be given to you" (Luke 6:38 NIV).

---

* https://www.investopedia.com/managing-wealth/worth-playing-lottery/

MY TAKEAWAYS:

1. How does this story challenge me?

2. How might I change this story in order to make it more relevant to my situation?

3. How can I reduce this story into one short sentence?

4. How do I hope others might respond to this story?

MEANT FOR ME

*T*hey were the most generous people we had ever known. While we weren't supposed to know, we were aware of a large gift they had given to our church. When we met at their home one Sunday evening for dessert, the topic of our pastor's recent sermon on giving was raised for discussion.

"I'm so glad we don't have to be troubled by that message." I said it smugly, wanting them to know that we were givers, too. The lesson was obviously directed at someone else, and I could only imagine how *those* people must have felt during the sermon.

Without blinking, he said, "I don't know. No matter how much I give, I always wonder if I'm doing all I should. God has been so good to us. I don't think I could ever give too much."

Before falling asleep that night, I had repented of my self-righteous pride and realized—of all people—that sermon was meant for me.

"But since you excel in everything—in faith, in speech, in knowledge, in complete earnestness and in the love we have kindled in you—see that you also excel in this grace of giving" (2 Corinthians 8:7 NIV).

MY TAKEAWAYS:

1. How does this story challenge me?

2. How might I change this story in order to make it more relevant to my situation?

3. How can I reduce this story into one short sentence?

4. How do I hope others might respond to this story?

FROM NOTHING TO EVERYTHING

*W*alter was a Bible school student in Buenos Aires, Argentina. In an evening chapel service, the speaker challenged the students to give a special offering for those soon departing on a mission trip. Walter knew he didn't have a single peso. Then, the speaker encouraged those with nothing to give to commit to give as the Lord provided the funds.

"I am committing to give the next money I receive as an offering for the mission trip," Walter told a fellow student. The student laughed and responded sarcastically, "Sure you will!"

At the conclusion of the service, Walter slipped out of his seat and went forward to pray. As he stood in prayer at the front of the chapel, someone pressed a 100-peso bill (about $25) into his hand. He immediately ran toward an usher and insisted they take his money and include it with the offering already being counted.

"Now he who supplies seed to the sower and bread for food..." (2 Corinthians 9:10 NIV).

Walter knows that Scripture to be true, and he believes the Lord provided him with the seed to sow. One moment he had nothing to give; moments later, he gave all that he had.

MY TAKEAWAYS:

1. How does this story challenge me?

2. How might I change this story in order to make it more relevant to my situation?

3. How can I reduce this story into one short sentence?

4. How do I hope others might respond to this story?

THE PARABLE OF THE SOWER

*D*o you remember the parable of the sower who scattered the seed in various places? Some fell along the path, some fell among the rocks, and other seeds fell among thorns. But the seed that fell on good soil produced a harvest with an exponential return.

The parable is not about money. Jesus explained the parable to His disciples in Luke 8:11: *"The seed is the word."* He did not promise a return on their money—He promised an exponential return on the sowing of the Word of God. Don't be frustrated because you haven't personally experienced a thirty-, sixty-, or hundredfold return on your giving. Instead, consider that giving honors God, advances the Kingdom, and changes eternal destinies.

The blessing of the Lord comes from trusting in Him and doing what He has instructed us. It may bring health, protection, provision, or a myriad of other rewards.

"'Bring the whole tithe into the storehouse, that there may be food in my house. Test me in this,' says the LORD Almighty, 'and see if I will not throw open the floodgates of heaven and pour out so much blessing that there will not be room enough to store it'" (Malachi 3:10 NIV).

MY TAKEAWAYS:

1. How does this story challenge me?

2. How might I change this story in order to make it more relevant to my situation?

3. How can I reduce this story into one short sentence?

4. How do I hope others might respond to this story?

GIVING WITH JOY

"*Each of you should give what you have decided in your heart to give, not reluctantly or under compulsion, for God loves a cheerful giver*" (2 Corinthians 9:7 NIV).

"Thank you for saying that," she said while pulling me aside after the morning service.

"What was it that I said?" I asked her with a puzzled look.

"What you said about giving. It's exactly what I needed to hear!"

The woman referred to my instructions about giving made prior to the offering. I simply stated, "If you're feeling coerced, please don't give. We do not need your money to the point that it's worth you giving with less than a cheerful heart."

Regular, methodical giving may be helpful for those living within a budget. But if a gift isn't given freely, with a cheerful attitude, then it was never really given. An amount was due. A payment was made. The transaction was complete and was taken away in plates or bags by people assigned to the task. There is no joy in that.

Give—with a cheerful heart and an open hand. God surely smiles upon us when we give in a way that reflects His character in our lives.

MY TAKEAWAYS:

1. How does this story challenge me?

2. How might I change this story in order to make it more relevant to my situation?

3. How can I reduce this story into one short sentence?

4. How do I hope others might respond to this story?

MARKET PERFORMANCE

$\mathcal{S}$uicide makes regular visits to Wall Street, but it's not only fund managers and stock traders who have been her victim through the years. Retired widows, housewives, and unemployed workers have believed suicide was the only answer to their investment losses. In California, forty-five-year-old Karthik Rajaram, an out-of-work money manager, took the lives of his wife, their three sons, and his mother-in-law before killing himself.*

Though stock markets did not exist at the time, everyone in ancient Israel had experienced drought, famine, pestilence, or disease in their lifetime. God's faithful provision made it possible for David to declare in Psalm 37:25, *"I was young and now I am old, yet I have never seen the righteous forsaken or their children begging bread"* (NIV).

Our lives are filled with disappointments, victories, tragedies, and triumphs. David's affirmation in the Psalms encourages us to see God's provision more like a tapestry than an individual thread. In the following verse, David writes, *"They are always generous and lend freely; their children will be a blessing"* (NIV).

Following after the Lord's instruction for generosity will lead us directly to His blessing. Our faithful God cares for us—and that's something not changed by market performance.

---

* www.huffingtonpost.com/2008/10/14/financial-crisis-suicide_n_134453.html

MY TAKEAWAYS:

1. How does this story challenge me?

2. How might I change this story in order to make it more relevant to my situation?

3. How can I reduce this story into one short sentence?

4. How do I hope others might respond to this story?

DIVIDENDS OF FAITHFULNESS

*I*t's the job of a performance coach to help their clients achieve otherwise unattainable goals. They push their clients to do more and cheer them on with motivational words and phrases like, "You can have it all—health, wealth, and relationships. Align your priorities. Shed those things holding you back. Tell yourself you are a winner. Do it now." Handclaps, shouts, and subtle amounts of shame are motivators used to get clients moving toward their personal success.

Performance coaches with a Christian perspective sometimes include this challenge: "You need to earn more so you can give more."

But that's not the way Jesus motivates us into generosity. From the richest to the poorest, Jesus makes it clear that faithful stewardship of our resources gives us the prospect of responsibility over even more.

Do you want to give more? Start by being faithful with the resources you have. The dividends paid by faithfulness will bless you with increased opportunities and the corresponding ability to bless others as a result.

"Well done, good and faithful servant! You have been faithful with a few things; I will put you in charge of many things. Come and share your master's happiness!" (Matthew 25:21, 23 NIV)

MY TAKEAWAYS:

1. How does this story challenge me?

2. How might I change this story in order to make it more relevant to my situation?

3. How can I reduce this story into one short sentence?

4. How do I hope others might respond to this story?

KING TUT'S TREASURES

*A*t nine years old, Tutankhamen (King Tut) became the pharaoh of Egypt. He died just ten years later. Though not a powerful or well-respected pharaoh, his name has become synonymous with the wealth of ancient Egypt.

After his death, a twenty-four-pound mask of gold and semi-precious stones were laid over Tutankhamen's face and upper torso. His mummified body was placed inside of three coffins. The first, made of solid gold, weighs 243 pounds. The outer two coffins are made of wood overlaid with gold. Another 5,000 items precious to the deceased pharaoh filled his burial chamber. An estimated value of the 2,640 pounds of just the gold in 2021 was near $85 million.

Not one piece of Tutankhamen's treasure accompanied him into the afterlife. Though it has traveled the world and been viewed by millions of people, none of his treasure ever helped to clothe or feed the hurting and hungry people he ruled.

Neither will our treasures accompany us. The Lord intends for them to make a difference today.

"Command those who are rich in this present world…to do good, to be rich in good deeds, and to be generous and willing to share" (1 Timothy 6:17–18 NIV).

MY TAKEAWAYS:

1. How does this story challenge me?

2. How might I change this story in order to make it more relevant to my situation?

3. How can I reduce this story into one short sentence?

4. How do I hope others might respond to this story?

ABOUNDING GRACE

"*And God is able to bless you abundantly, so that in all things at all times, having all that you need, you will abound in every good work*" (2 Corinthians 9:8 NIV).

The Greek word for "abound" (*perisseuō*) can be translated to mean, *"having more than you at first assumed."* By all calculations and based upon the best available information at the time, a certain amount should have been available. But in the end, after the accounting was done, an extra amount was on hand.

It's what happens when God's blessing comes to us. The things we deserve the least are what we receive (especially things like grace, mercy, love, and forgiveness) in a measure beyond our expectations. We did nothing to deserve them, nor anything to earn them. They are gifts from God, who loves to lavish them on His children (1 John 3:1). In turn, the way He expresses His love toward us should cause us to express grace, mercy, love, and forgiveness to others.

What joy it must bring our heavenly Father when we bless others without thought of repayment or reward. In fact, it brings Him so much joy that He blesses us again and again.

MY TAKEAWAYS:

1. How does this story challenge me?

2. How might I change this story in order to make it more relevant to my situation?

3. How can I reduce this story into one short sentence?

4. How do I hope others might respond to this story?

COVERING ALL THE BASES

*M*ethods of giving are different today than in previous years. Recent surveys estimate that many adults carry little, if any, cash. Instead, they prefer giving with credit/debit cards, texting, or with mobile apps. It is increasingly necessary to consider how to facilitate giving without overlooking the reasons why we give.

Our pastor recently referred to a graphic in a media presentation that provided instructions on "Three Ways to Give." The methods were clearly listed:

1. Check—Payable to "First Church"
2. Cash—Envelopes at the end of each row
3. Online—With credit/debit card, text, or by app

He also provided the church's website address for those interested in giving online.

At first glance, it appeared our pastor had covered all the bases. Then, he wisely instructed us beyond the mechanics and into the spirit of giving.

"There are at least three other ways you should give," he continued. "Those other ways are cheerfully, generously, and expectantly. Those three should always be at the top of our list."

While our methods of giving may change, the message about giving remains the same for us today. Jesus made it clear: *"It is more blessed to give than to receive"* (Acts 20:35 NIV).

MY TAKEAWAYS:

1. How does this story challenge me?

2. How might I change this story in order to make it more relevant to my situation?

3. How can I reduce this story into one short sentence?

4. How do I hope others might respond to this story?

WHAT CAESAR IS DUE

$\mathcal{N}$o one is certain how many taxpayers are guilty of tax evasion each year. The IRS estimates that $1 trillion of tax revenue was lost in 2020 from tax evasion. Had it been collected, those taxes would have covered about ten weeks of government expenses that fiscal year.

What kind of person would not pay taxes? It isn't just big corporate moneymakers and unscrupulous politicians. It's many little guys along the way, too. Like those who receive cash for jobs performed with no paper trail connecting their work to their income. It's those who hire people to work in their homes and those who work in others' homes. Some people don't report their tips while others claim business trip expenses that are actually vacations.

Few are ever caught. Those who do get caught are typically the prominent who owe large amounts of money. The rest get away with it.

Really?

Jesus told His followers in Matthew 22:21, *"Give back to Caesar what is Caesar's, and to God what is God's"* (NIV).

We are called to be exemplary citizens of both heaven and earth. Being generous givers and conscientious taxpayers brings glory to God and opens the path for His blessing.

MY TAKEAWAYS:

1. How does this story challenge me?

2. How might I change this story in order to make it more relevant to my situation?

3. How can I reduce this story into one short sentence?

4. How do I hope others might respond to this story?

PROVEN STEWARDS

"*Because of the service by which you have proved yourselves, others will praise God for the obedience that accompanies your confession of the gospel of Christ, and for your generosity in sharing with them and with everyone else*" (2 Corinthians 9:13 NIV).

The number of seeds planted and harvested in a given area is called a "crop yield." In order to maximize the harvest, seed must be planted at proper intervals. One type of seed may require different spacing, moisture, or sunlight than another.

It is important to know where the seed you share in ministry is being planted. Although you may not know the final point of distribution, knowing the one to whom you have trusted your seed is essential. For example:

- Is there a history of good stewardship?
- Is there a verifiable record of their ministry activities?
- Are regular updates on their activities provided to donors?
- Do they provide timely acknowledgments of the gifts received?

When sharing valuable resources the Lord has entrusted to you, take care to invest in those you know and trust. The blessing you receive from wise giving will make it possible for you to give again with confidence in the days to come.

MY TAKEAWAYS:

1. How does this story challenge me?

2. How might I change this story in order to make it more relevant to my situation?

3. How can I reduce this story into one short sentence?

4. How do I hope others might respond to this story?

DON'T TAKE MY GIFT

*P*erhaps it matters only to me. Maybe it's just semantics, but I cringe when I hear the words, *"The ushers are coming to take your offering."*

Not because I am opposed to giving in the offering. I make every attempt to be prepared to give when I go to church. That's because I believe giving is an integral part of worship, and worship comes from my heart. I go to church expecting to worship and to give. I know the Lord is blessed by both—and I am, too.

In other words, ushers should not be instructed to "take my worship." Instead, they should be instructed to receive my gift brought to the Lord. They should receive it with reverence and honor. Not for me, but because of that which is due to the Lord.

Please—don't "take" my offering. When you do, it becomes increasingly difficult for me to give it. And giving, with a cheerful heart, is the very basis of how we are taught to give.

God instructed Moses to, *"tell the Israelites to bring me an offering. You are to receive the offering for me from everyone whose heart prompts them to give"* (Exodus 25:2 NIV).

MY TAKEAWAYS:

1. How does this story challenge me?

2. How might I change this story in order to make it more relevant to my situation?

3. How can I reduce this story into one short sentence?

4. How do I hope others might respond to this story?

NO INCREASE

A recent six-month period saw dramatic increases in retail prices. Unleaded gasoline saw rises of more than $1 per gallon. Grocery prices climbed about 15 percent over the same time period. The price of used vehicles was up nearly 50 percent, and lumber prices tripled in some areas.

Robert Orben, a comedian and onetime presidential speechwriter, once made this observation: "Inflation is bringing us true democracy. For the first time in history, luxuries and necessities are selling at the same price."

In the midst of uncertain economic times, there is still good news for us! Since first instituted some four thousand years ago, the tithe percentage has never been increased; it remains at 10 percent. Neither has God's promise to bless those who are generous changed at all. The promises found in His Word are not subject to the times and seasons in which we live.

"Bring the whole tithe into the storehouse, that there may be food in my house. Test me in this," says the LORD Almighty, "and see if I will not throw open the floodgates of heaven and pour out so much blessing that there will not be room enough to store it" (Malachi 3:10 NIV).

MY TAKEAWAYS:

1. How does this story challenge me?

2. How might I change this story in order to make it more relevant to my situation?

3. How can I reduce this story into one short sentence?

4. How do I hope others might respond to this story?

"OUR PEOPLE ARE POOR"

I've heard it spoken often from leaders of Christian communities in some of the world's most impoverished nations. I know why they're poor, and it has nothing to do with their nation's economy. Neither does it have to do with the marginalized status Christians hold in their society.

I typically hear the statement after asking, "Pastor, do you teach your people to tithe?" Their response is typical, and I know exactly what will come next. Someday, I'll write down the answer before they give it, but will wait to show it until they answer.

They are poor because the leadership has been too afraid to tell the truth. Perhaps it's too hard to believe, or maybe it is because they will be accused of seeking personal gain. But the truth is still true.

"The generous will themselves be blessed" (Proverbs 22:9 NIV), and *"The blessing of the LORD brings wealth"* (Proverbs 10:22 NIV).

While you may not be able to wish yourself out of poverty, it is apparent that you can give your way into blessing. It is more than a onetime event that leads to riches. It is a way of life that leads to having more than enough.

MY TAKEAWAYS:

1. How does this story challenge me?

2. How might I change this story in order to make it more relevant to my situation?

3. How can I reduce this story into one short sentence?

4. How do I hope others might respond to this story?

SUPPORTING COMMUNITY MISSIONS

*S*ome believe missions can only be described for activities in distant lands where people speak other languages and adopt different cultural practices. But have you considered how giving to a local church can also be deemed a mission activity?

Pastors and church staff members find outreach opportunities in hospitals and high schools, in nursing homes and to the homebound. They serve on community and church boards and work with bored kids. Whether the people to whom they minister are infants or invalids, hungry or homeless, they are responding to the mandate of Christ to *"go into all the world and preach the gospel to all creation"* (Mark 16:15 NIV). Men, women, young adults, teenagers, and children—all provide opportunities for sharing the love of Jesus.

Utility payments, capital improvements, salaries, and office supplies don't share the same glamour as caring for orphans and widows, building churches in the heart of Africa, translating the Scriptures, or reaching the multitudes with mass media. But the pastors and staff members of local churches believe that community ministry is a mandate and fulfill the Great Commission right where they live, and our giving is one of the most important tools that make it possible.

MY TAKEAWAYS:

1. How does this story challenge me?

2. How might I change this story in order to make it more relevant to my situation?

3. How can I reduce this story into one short sentence?

4. How do I hope others might respond to this story?

MISPLACED VALUES

"*Do not store up for yourselves treasures on earth, where moth and rust destroy, and where thieves break in and steal. But store up for yourselves treasures in heaven, where neither moth nor rust destroys, and where thieves do not break in or steal*" (Matthew 6:19–21).

This Scripture may seem confusing (even contradictory) to teachings in other passages. In 1 Timothy 5, Paul instructs us to provide for our own household. Then, in the very next chapter, he tells us to enjoy the good things given to us while hoping in God, not our own wealth. And Proverbs 6 commends work and encourages setting aside provision for the future.

So, shall we save money for the future or give it all away?

Jesus' concern was about the selfishness found in misplaced values. As His disciples, we must honestly ask ourselves where our motivations lie. Clearly, Kingdom investments give a greater anticipation of Kingdom advancements.

We are not called to be hoarders or materialists who always want more. Neither are we prohibited from setting aside provision for the future. Both giving and saving honors God, provides for the ministries of the church, and helps us to prepare for the future.

MY TAKEAWAYS:

1. How does this story challenge me?

2. How might I change this story in order to make it more relevant to my situation?

3. How can I reduce this story into one short sentence?

4. How do I hope others might respond to this story?

RELEASING MIRACLES

*H*ave you considered the responsibility of the ushers who receive our offerings? It occurs to me that they collect more than cash, checks, coins, or other commitments as they walk the aisles.

From some, they receive gifts of thanksgiving. Others bring their tithe and the steadfast hope that God will pour out blessings upon them. Some will give more than they planned while others may give all that is left. In the bags the ushers carry are found expressions of hope and trust mixed in with desperate prayers for help.

Ushers not only receive these gifts on behalf of the church, but they also accept them on behalf of the Kingdom of God. He doesn't need our money, but He does desire our hearts. He knows that where we place our treasures, our hearts will not be far behind. Though ushers may collect money in those bags, they are also helping to release miracles through the duty they perform.

Ushers, as you walk the aisles, pray for those in the churches you serve. Pray that God will release the miracles people need. Pray that healing, hope, deliverance, and restoration will come to those who release their faith as they give.

MY TAKEAWAYS:

1. How does this story challenge me?

2. How might I change this story in order to make it more relevant to my situation?

3. How can I reduce this story into one short sentence?

4. How do I hope others might respond to this story?

GOD'S COWBOY

(ADAPTED FROM A STORY BY
DR. NORMAN LINDSAY)

*S*hortly after it was founded in 1924, Dallas Theological Seminary was near bankruptcy. Creditors planned to foreclose at noon on a particular day. That morning, faculty members met in the office of the president, Dr. Chafer, to pray for God's provision. When it was his turn, Dr. Harry Ironside prayed: *"Lord, we know the cattle on a thousand hills are Thine. Please sell some of them and send us the money."*

As they prayed, a tall Texan with boots and an open collar stepped up to the business office and said, *"I just sold two carloads of cattle in Fort Worth, and I feel compelled to give the money to the seminary."*

A secretary brought the man's check to the prayer meeting. Dr. Chafer took the check out of her hand and found it was exactly the amount of their debt. He turned to Dr. Ironside and said, *"Harry, God sold the cattle!"**

God's promises are not only for others, although He often works through the generosity of others to bring about the miracles we need at just the right time.

"God will meet all your needs according to the riches of his glory in Christ Jesus" (Philippians 4:19 NIV).

---

*James S. Hewett, *Illustrations Unlimited* (Wheaton: Tyndale House Publishers, Inc, 1988), 419.

MY TAKEAWAYS:

1. How does this story challenge me?

2. How might I change this story in order to make it more relevant to my situation?

3. How can I reduce this story into one short sentence?

4. How do I hope others might respond to this story?

AUTHENTIC GIVERS

As the associate pastor, I attended each of our three Sunday morning services. Since the pastoral staff was seated on the platform before the entire congregation, the senior pastor encouraged us to be "models" of giving. When the offering bag was passed, everyone would see us place our offering in it. We all agreed it was a good idea.

However, the plan and my practice were not the same. Rather than write three separate checks each Sunday, I normally put blank, empty envelopes in two of the three offerings.

Could others have questioned my integrity? What blessing can be found when giving nothing? Though the Lord saw my heart, the only thing others saw was my wish to be seen by them as a generous giver.

When we give to be noticed by others, their recognition is our reward. Authentic givers seek only to be noticed by the Lord. Being discreet and generous are not mutually exclusive terms. It is the way we have been instructed to give.

"Be careful not to practice your righteousness in front of others to be seen by them. If you do, you will have no reward from your Father in heaven" (Matthew 6:1 NIV).

MY TAKEAWAYS:

1. How does this story challenge me?

2. How might I change this story in order to make it more relevant to my situation?

3. How can I reduce this story into one short sentence?

4. How do I hope others might respond to this story?

ABOUT THE AUTHOR

Ric Shields is a follower of Jesus who loves his wife and family. He enjoys writing, especially about life experiences from growing up on a farm in eastern Iowa, to the villages of Bangladesh, the heart of Egypt, twenty-nine countries on six continents, and countless places in between.

He is the founder and director of **DoorWays®** and the *Leadership and Influence Network,* and he believes the call to ministry is experienced by many more than those who embrace it vocationally.

Dr. Shields is the recipient of the Oral Roberts University Outstanding Biology and Chemistry Department Alumnus (2013–2014) and a Doctor of Humane Letters from Logos University (2015).

You may contact Ric Shields at:

DoorWays®
PO Box 2023
Broken Arrow, OK 74013

Email: info@doorways.cc